UNDER THE MICROSCOPE

Making Life

How we reproduce and grow

Contributors

Author and series consultant: **Richard Walker BSc PhD PGCE** taught biology, science, and health education for several years before becoming a full-time writer. He is a foremost author and consultant specializing in books for adults and children on human biology, health, and natural history. He is the author of *Heart: How the blood gets around the body, Making Life: How we reproduce and grow, Muscles: How we move and exercise,* and *Brain: Our body's nerve center* in this series, and is consultant on the whole series.

Advisory panel

1 Heart: How the blood gets around the body
P. M. Schofield MD FRCP FICA FACC FESC is Consultant Cardiologist at Papworth Hospital, Cambridge, UK

2 Skeleton: Our body's framework
R. N. Villar MS FRCS is Consultant Orthopedic Surgeon at Cambridge BUPA Lea Hospital and Addenbrooke's Hospital, Cambridge, UK

3 Digesting: How we fuel the body
J. O. Hunter FRCP is Director of the Gastroenterology Research Unit, Addenbrooke's Hospital, Cambridge, UK

4 Making Life: How we reproduce and grow
Jane MacDougall MD MRCOG is Consultant Obstetrician and Gynecologist at the Rosie Maternity Hospital, Addenbrooke's NHS Trust, Cambridge, UK

5 Breathing: How we use air
Mark Slade MA MBBS MRCP is Senior Registrar, Department of Respiratory Medicine, Addenbrooke's Hospital, Cambridge, UK

6 Senses: How we connect with the world
Peter Garrard MA MRCP is Medical Research Council Fellow and Honorary Specialist Registrar, Neurology Department, Addenbrooke's Hospital, Cambridge, UK

7 Muscles: How we move and exercise
Jumbo Jenner MD FRCP is Consultant, and **R. T. Kavanagh MD MRCP** is Senior Registrar, Department of Rheumatology, Addenbrooke's Hospital, Cambridge, UK

8 Brain: Our body's nerve center
Peter Garrard MA MRCP is Medical Research Council Fellow and Honorary Specialist Registrar, Neurology Department, Addenbrooke's Hospital, Cambridge, UK

Making Life

How we reproduce and grow

Richard Walker

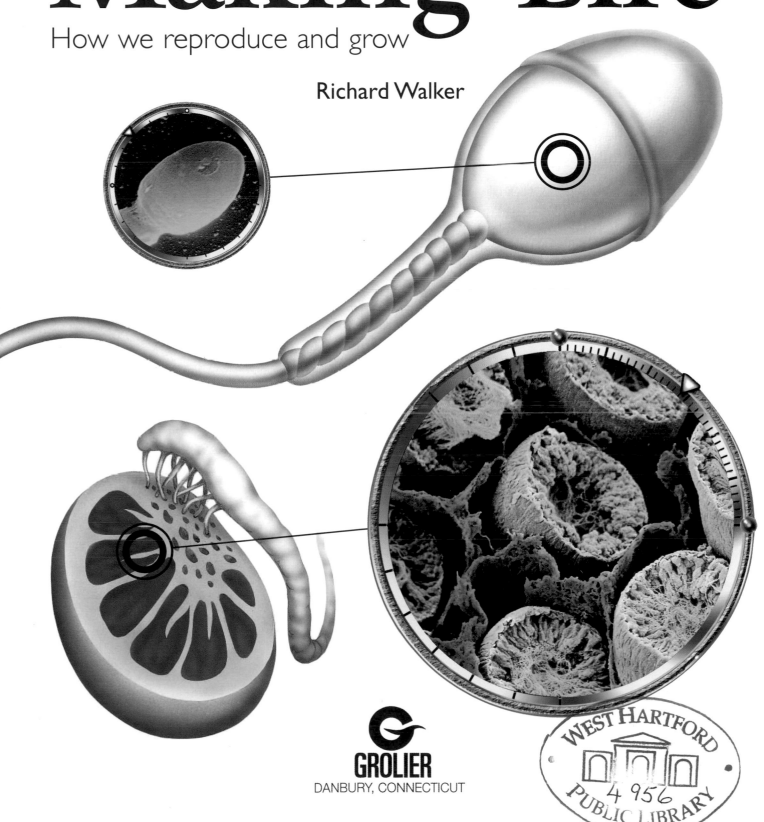

GROLIER

DANBURY, CONNECTICUT

Printed in 2005

GROLIER
DANBURY, CONNECTICUT

First published in 1998 by
Grolier Educational
Sherman Turnpike
Danbury
Connecticut

Set ISBN 0-7172-9265-7
Volume ISBN 0-7172-9269-X

Library of Congress Cataloging-in-Publication Data

Under the microscope : the human body
    p.   cm.
  Includes bibliographical references and index
  Contents: v. 1. Skeleton - v. 2. Brain - v. 3. Heart - v. 4. Making life - v. 5. Senses - v. 6. Digesting - v. 7. Muscles - v. 8. Breathing.
  ISBN 0-7172-9265-7 (set)
  1. Human physiology - Juvenile literature. 2. Human anatomy - Juvenile literature. 3. Body, Human - Juvenile literature. [1. Human physiology. 2. Human anatomy. 3. Body, Human.]
  I. Grolier Educational (Firm)
QP37.U53 1998
612–DC21
97-38977
CIP
AC

Produced by Franklin Watts
96 Leonard Street
London EC2A 4RH

Creative development by
Miles Kelly Publishing
Unit 11
The Bardfield Centre
Great Bardfield
Essex CM7 4SL

Printed in China

Designed by Full Steam Ahead

Illustrated by Roger Gorringe

Artwork commissioning: Branka Surla

ABOUT THIS BOOK

Under the Microscope uses microphotography to allow you to see right inside the human body.

The camera acts as a microscope, looking at unseen parts of the body and zooming in on the body's cells at work. Some microphotographs are magnified hundreds of times, others thousands of times. They have been dramatically colored to bring details into crisp focus and are linked to clear and accurate illustrations that fit them in context inside the body.

New words are explained the first time that they are used and can also be checked in the glossary at the back of the book, which includes a helpful pronunciation guide.

Sperm factory
This micrograph shows tiny sperm with their round "heads" and long tails in the process of being made. Sperm are produced in part of the male reproductive system, the testes.

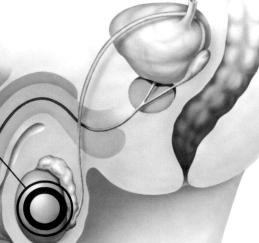

JQ
612
UNDER ?
v.4
J
11/05

4

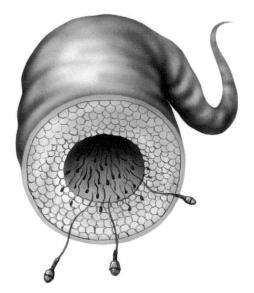

CONTENTS

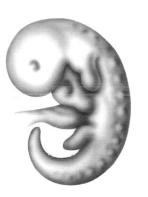

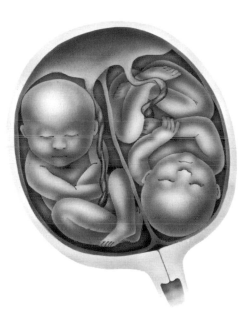

INTRODUCTION

A new life

Six days after a sperm meets an egg, a future human being looks like this. Made up of just a few cells, this brand new life is about to attach itself to the inside of its mother's womb.

While you are reading this, it could be happening in Bangalore, India, or Toronto, Canada. Or, perhaps, in Riyadh, Saudi Arabia, or Osaka, Japan, or Oxford, England. The "it" that might be happening is the birth of a baby. Or, rather, babies. Because during the next minute, around the world, 170 babies will be born.

Having babies is a natural part of human life. It is also something that humans have in common with all living things from microscopic bacteria to gigantic blue whales. None of us can live forever. By having babies, we produce our successors – and make sure that our species does not die out. The remarkable process by which all this happens is called reproduction. And the part of the body involved with reproduction is called the reproductive system.

The reproductive system is present inside our body when we are born. But it only starts working when we reach our teens. Men and women's reproductive systems look different, but they have the same basic job to do. They both produce special cells called sex cells. If a man's and a woman's sex cells meet, they join together and develop into a new human being. After nine months growing and developing inside its mother, the baby is ready to be born.

Each one of the 250,000 babies born today, and every day, started life in the same way: the joining together of two microscopic sex cells. This book tells the remarkable story of how two tiny sex cells make a baby. And how that baby grows into a child and then an adult.

EMERGING EGG

Like an erupting volcano, an egg bursts out from a woman's ovary (right). Although it looks large here, the egg is smaller than the period at the end of this sentence.

Looking human

Above is the face of a tiny baby that has been growing inside its mother for eight weeks. At this stage the baby is called a fetus. Already it looks human.

Chromosomes

These are chromosomes, tiny structures found inside every one of the body's cells. Chromosomes carry the instructions needed to make and operate a living human being.

6

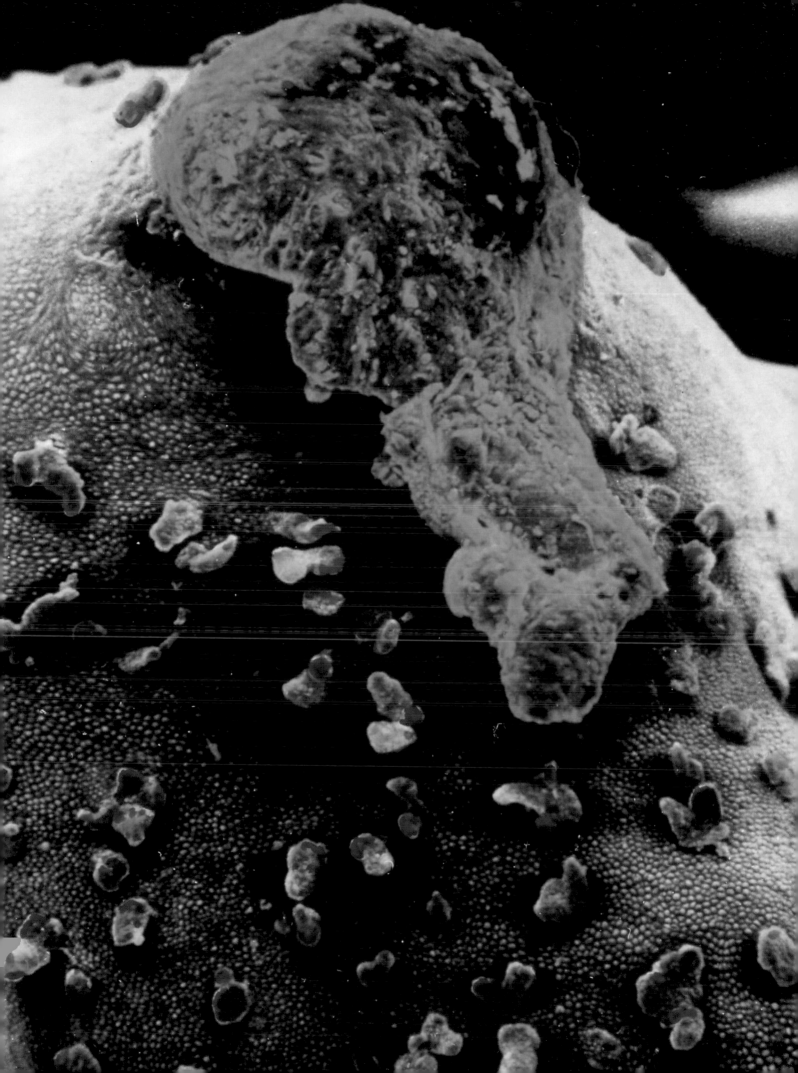

THE FEMALE REPRODUCTIVE SYSTEM

A woman's reproductive system has three jobs to do. It stores and releases female sex cells called eggs or ova. It provides a place where an egg and sperm (male sex cell) can meet to produce a new baby. And it protects and feeds the new baby while it is developing inside its mother.

Two ovaries, each the size of an almond, produce, store, and release eggs. About two million immature, or unripe, eggs are made by a girl's ovaries before she is born, and stored. From the time she reaches puberty, at around the age of 12, one egg is released each month. If an egg meets a sperm, it develops into a baby inside a woman's uterus. This has muscular, stretchy walls and swells as the baby grows.

Inside a breast

The breasts are not part of the reproductive system. But they are important after the birth of a baby because they produce milk. A woman's breast contains mammary (milk-producing) glands. These are surrounded by fat. The more fat there is inside the breast, the larger it is. When a woman gives birth to her baby, the mammary glands release milk. This travels along ducts (tubes) that open through the nipple.

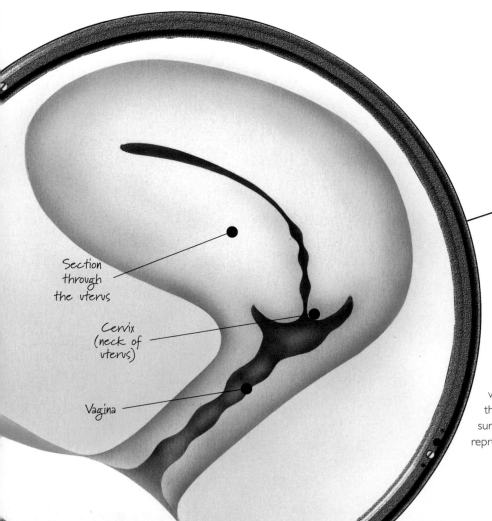

Section through the uterus

Cervix (neck of uterus)

Vagina

Uterus and vagina

This is a section through a woman's reproductive system. The uterus is a hollow organ that is about the same size as its owner's fist. The cervix, or neck, of the uterus opens into the vagina. This leads to the outside of the body. The vagina opens just behind the opening of the urinary system through which urine passes when a girl or woman goes to the bathroom. The vaginal and urinary openings are surrounded by the vulva, the outside part of the reproductive system.

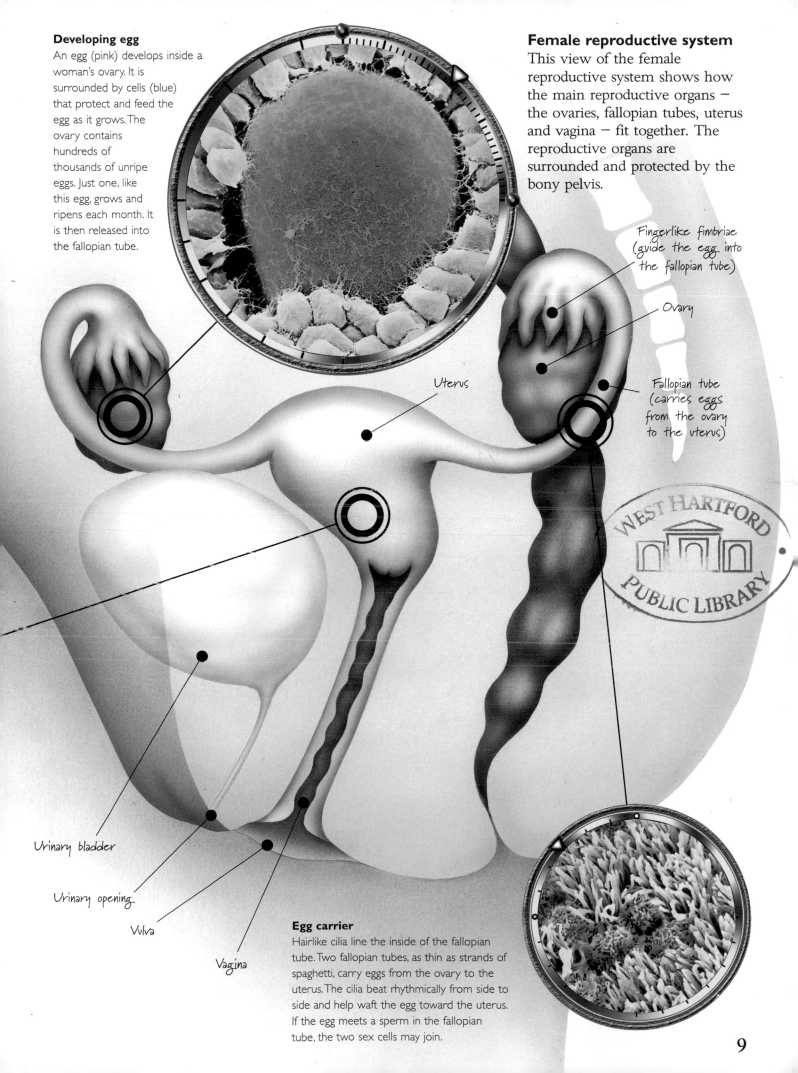

Developing egg
An egg (pink) develops inside a woman's ovary. It is surrounded by cells (blue) that protect and feed the egg as it grows. The ovary contains hundreds of thousands of unripe eggs. Just one, like this egg, grows and ripens each month. It is then released into the fallopian tube.

Female reproductive system
This view of the female reproductive system shows how the main reproductive organs — the ovaries, fallopian tubes, uterus and vagina — fit together. The reproductive organs are surrounded and protected by the bony pelvis.

Fingerlike fimbriae (guide the egg into the fallopian tube)

Ovary

Uterus

Fallopian tube (carries eggs from the ovary to the uterus)

Urinary bladder

Urinary opening

Vulva

Vagina

Egg carrier
Hairlike cilia line the inside of the fallopian tube. Two fallopian tubes, as thin as strands of spaghetti, carry eggs from the ovary to the uterus. The cilia beat rhythmically from side to side and help waft the egg toward the uterus. If the egg meets a sperm in the fallopian tube, the two sex cells may join.

THE MENSTRUAL CYCLE

From her early teens to her early fifties a woman releases an egg from one of her ovaries each month. At the same time, her uterus prepares to receive the egg if it is fertilized (joined with a sperm). The changes that occur each month in the uterus are called the menstrual cycle.

Where is it?
The uterus and ovaries are located in the lower part of the abdomen (the part of the body between the chest and the legs). They are surrounded by the protective ring of the pelvic girdle, or hip bones.

The word "menstrual" means monthly. Something is described as a "cycle" if it always follows the same sequence of events and repeats itself regularly.

Hormones are chemical messengers carried by the blood. They control many body activities, including the menstrual cycle. Each month hormones are released from the pituitary gland, found just below the brain. These hormones cause one unripe egg to mature each month and be released from the ovary. This is called ovulation. At the same time, hormones released by the ovary cause the inner lining of the uterus to thicken. This happens so that a fertilized egg can sink into the lining and develop into a baby. If fertilization does not occur — and most months it does not — the thickened lining breaks down and passes out through the vagina. This is called a period, or menstruation.

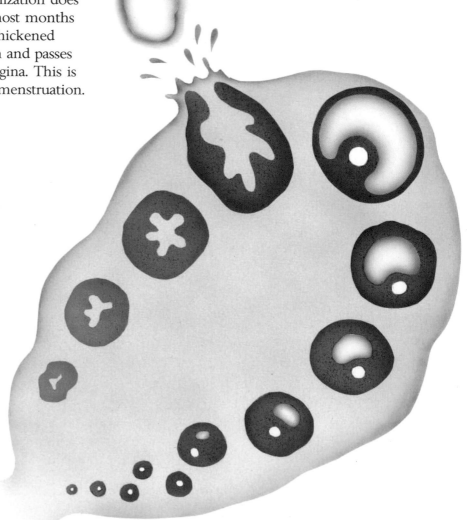

Monthly changes
Each month the same sequence of changes happens in a woman's ovaries and uterus to prepare her body for pregnancy. The only time that monthly changes do not happen is if the woman is pregnant. On average, the menstrual cycle lasts for 28 days, but it can be longer or shorter.

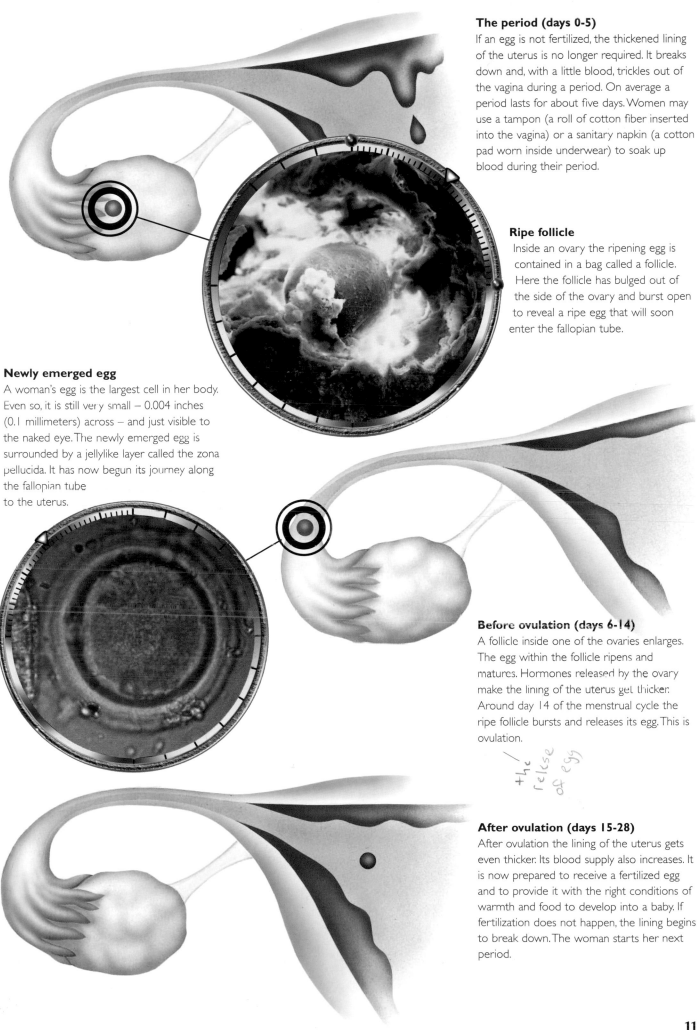

The period (days 0-5)

If an egg is not fertilized, the thickened lining of the uterus is no longer required. It breaks down and, with a little blood, trickles out of the vagina during a period. On average a period lasts for about five days. Women may use a tampon (a roll of cotton fiber inserted into the vagina) or a sanitary napkin (a cotton pad worn inside underwear) to soak up blood during their period.

Ripe follicle

Inside an ovary the ripening egg is contained in a bag called a follicle. Here the follicle has bulged out of the side of the ovary and burst open to reveal a ripe egg that will soon enter the fallopian tube.

Newly emerged egg

A woman's egg is the largest cell in her body. Even so, it is still very small – 0.004 inches (0.1 millimeters) across – and just visible to the naked eye. The newly emerged egg is surrounded by a jellylike layer called the zona pellucida. It has now begun its journey along the fallopian tube to the uterus.

Before ovulation (days 6-14)

A follicle inside one of the ovaries enlarges. The egg within the follicle ripens and matures. Hormones released by the ovary make the lining of the uterus get thicker. Around day 14 of the menstrual cycle the ripe follicle bursts and releases its egg. This is ovulation.

the relese of egg

After ovulation (days 15-28)

After ovulation the lining of the uterus gets even thicker. Its blood supply also increases. It is now prepared to receive a fertilized egg and to provide it with the right conditions of warmth and food to develop into a baby. If fertilization does not happen, the lining begins to break down. The woman starts her next period.

THE MALE REPRODUCTIVE SYSTEM

A man's reproductive system, like a woman's, starts working when he is in his early teens. It has two main roles. First, it produces sperm, the male sex cells. Second, it transports sperm from where they are made and deposits them inside a woman's reproductive system. When this happens, fertilization may take place.

The two testes are oval-shaped organs. They produce sperm and hang outside the body in a bag of skin called the scrotum. Running around part of each testis is a tube called the epididymis. This is where sperm are stored as they mature. A sperm duct, or ductus deferens, runs from each epididymis around the side of the urinary bladder. The two sperm ducts join just below the bladder and link up with the urethra. This is a tube that runs to the outside of the body along the penis.

The penis, which is a tube-shaped organ, also hangs outside the body. It is filled with spongy tissue. If the spongy tissue fills with blood, the penis becomes longer and stiffer. This is an erection. When this happens, a man is able gently to push his penis into his partner's vagina. This is called sexual intercourse. It enables sperm to pass from the man's reproductive system to the woman's. If an egg has recently been released by the woman's ovary, it may be fertilized by a sperm.

Where is it?
The male reproductive system is at the bottom of the abdomen. Part of it is inside the body, but the penis and testes hang outside.

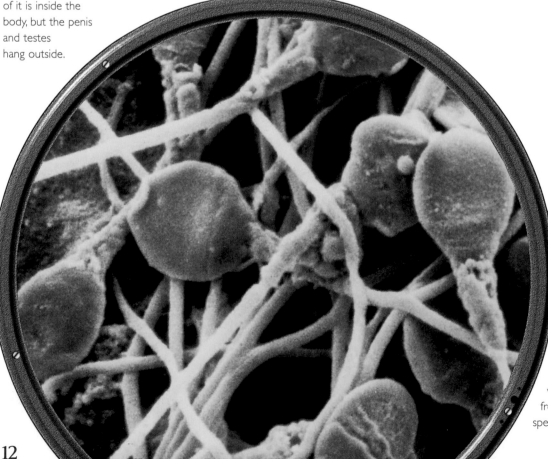

Streamlined swimmers
This micrograph clearly shows the heads and tails of several sperm inside the testis. The sperm's head is oval and flattened. This makes the sperm more streamlined so that it can move through liquids with ease. The long tail lashes from side to side to push the sperm forward.

Male reproductive system

The testes and penis hang outside the body at the top of the legs. Sperm ducts carry sperm from the testes to the penis. The male reproductive and urinary systems are linked together. Both share the urethra, the tube that runs from the bladder (which stores urine) to the outside of the body along the penis.

Bladder

Seminal vesicles (produce semen)

Prostate gland (also produces semen)

Sperm duct

Penis

Urethra

Epididymis

Testis

Scrotum

Young sperm
Easily identified by their long tails, these young sperm are developing inside the testis, the body's sperm factory. The cells surrounding the young sperm provide them with food while they are developing.

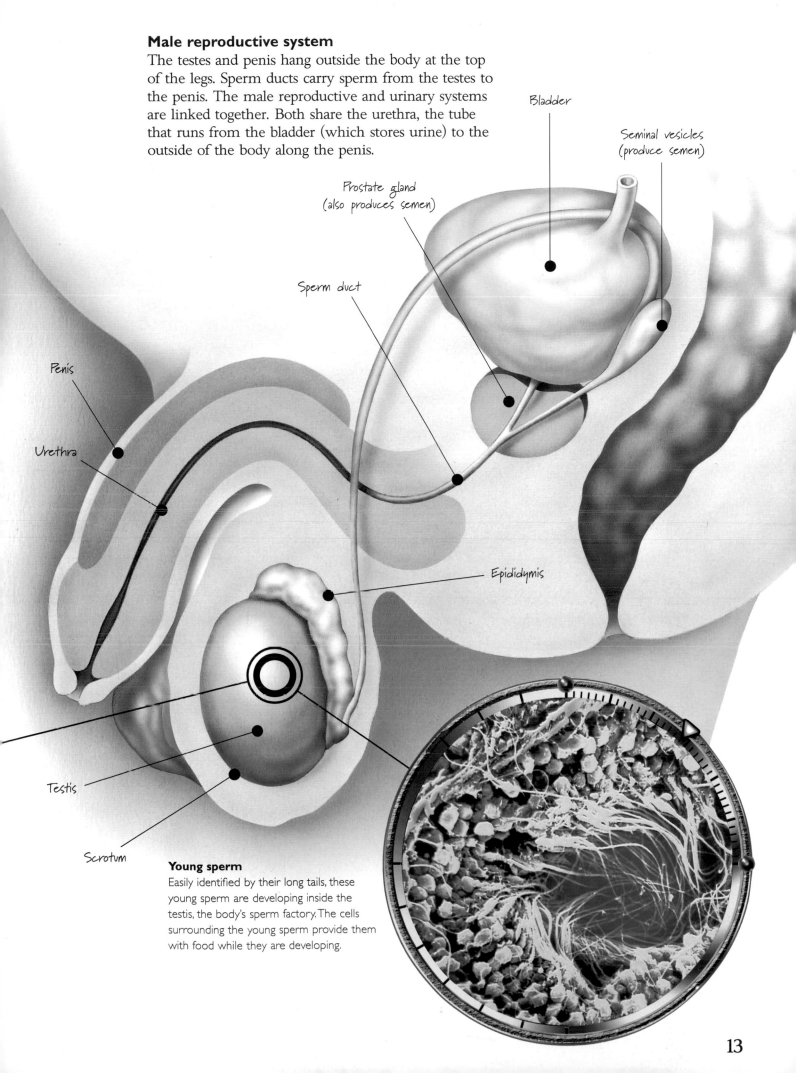

MAKING SPERM

Sperm are made inside the testes. Sperm production is controlled by hormones (chemical messengers) released from the pituitary gland below the brain. Other hormones produced by the testes themselves are also needed. Men produce sperm from their early teens into old age. This contrasts with women, who produce all their eggs before they are born and then release them, one each month, from their teens until their early fifties.

Sperm are manufactured by a mass of tiny tubes inside the testes. Over 1,000 sperm are produced every second, and more than 100 million every day. When a man ejaculates – this means he releases sperm from his penis – between 300 and 500 million sperm are released. If sperm are not released, they are recycled. The testes that make the sperm are outside the body in the scrotum for a good reason. Normal body temperature (98.6°Fahrenheit or 37°Centigrade) is too hot for sperm production. In the scrotum it is about 5°Fahrenheit (3°Centigrade) lower than normal, ideal for making sperm. In cold weather muscles pull the scrotum closer to the body to ensure the testes do not get too cool.

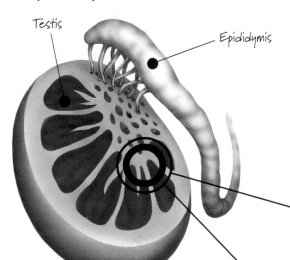

Testis

Epididymis

Parts of a sperm
A sperm has three parts. The head contains a nucleus. This carries some of the instructions needed to make a new human being. The tail, or flagellum, moves from side to side to push the sperm forward. The midpiece supplies the energy needed for movement.

Inside a testis
Each testis is packed with over a thousand tiny tubes called seminiferous tubules. Sperm pass from the seminiferous tubule into the epididymis. This is where maturing sperm are stored.

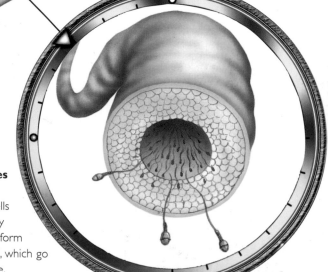

Seminiferous tubules
Inside each tubule is a sperm-production line. Cells inside the tubule constantly divide into two. New cells form sperm, complete with a tail, which go to the epididymis to mature.

Sperm

Sperm are tadpolelike cells with a streamlined shape. They are much smaller than eggs — just 0.002 inches (0.05 millimeters) long. Unlike eggs, sperm can move actively. They swim using their whiplike tails.

Massed tails

The microscope reveals a mass of sperm tails inside a seminiferous tubule. Sperm start off as rounded cells, but during their development they become long and thin. This makes them lighter and faster moving.

Sperm factories

This remarkable micrograph shows the cut ends of seminiferous tubules inside a man's testis. Inside each tubule is a swirl of developing sperm (blue). Each sperm takes about 10 weeks to produce. Around the tubules are cells (orange) that release hormones that help control sperm production.

FERTILIZATION

Fertilization is the joining together of a sperm and an egg, an action that produces a new human life.

A man releases sperm into a woman's vagina during sexual intercourse. This is a very personal and intimate act between two people. A man moves his penis inside his partner's vagina until he ejaculates, and the sperm are released. Millions of sperm are ejaculated, but only a few continue their journey. Beating their tails, they swim through the cervix, into the uterus and on toward the fallopian tubes. This hazardous journey is equivalent to a person swimming 4.5 miles (7 kilometers) in a choppy sea. If an egg is present in one of the fallopian tubes, one sperm fuses with it and fertilizes it. As the fertilized egg continues its journey toward the uterus, the first stages of development into a baby take place.

If a couple want to avoid having a baby, they may use a contraceptive. A contraceptive stops a sperm from meeting an egg.

Where it happens

Fertilization takes place in a woman's body, when sperm and egg meet in the fallopian tube.

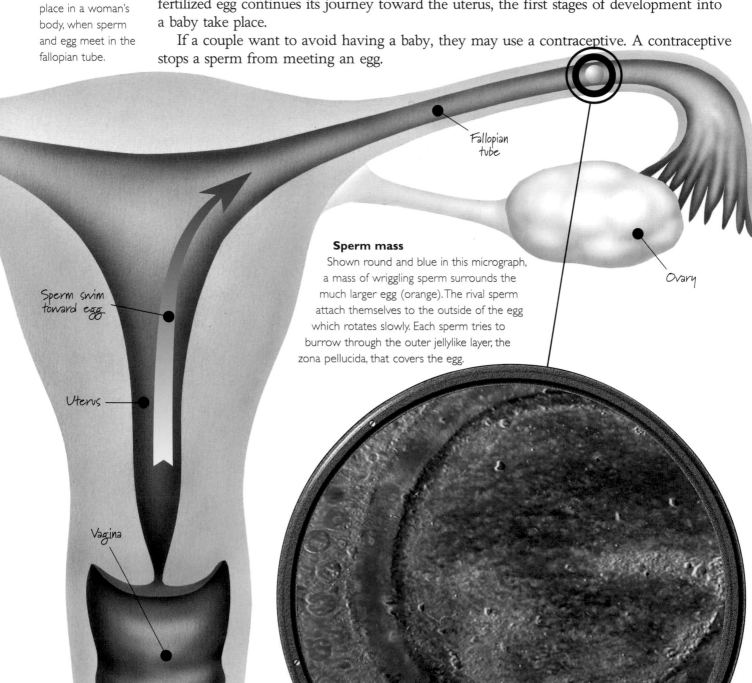

Fallopian tube

Ovary

Sperm mass
Shown round and blue in this micrograph, a mass of wriggling sperm surrounds the much larger egg (orange). The rival sperm attach themselves to the outside of the egg which rotates slowly. Each sperm tries to burrow through the outer jellylike layer, the zona pellucida, that covers the egg.

Sperm swim toward egg

Uterus

Vagina

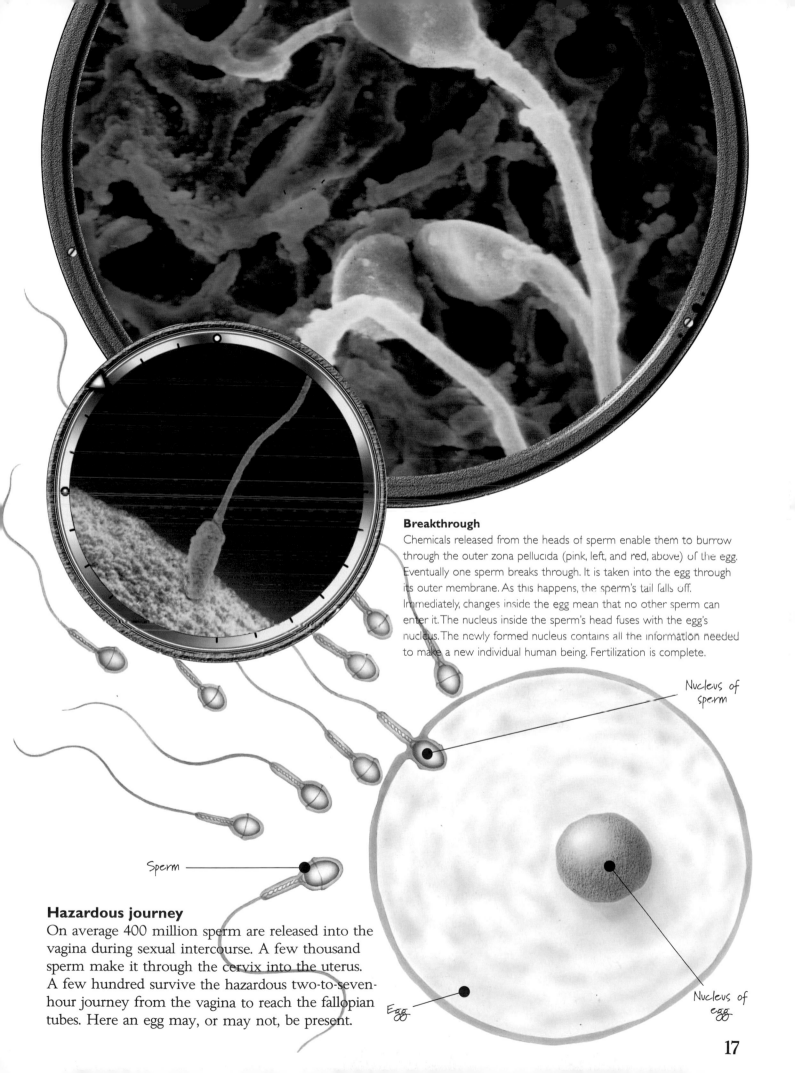

Breakthrough

Chemicals released from the heads of sperm enable them to burrow through the outer zona pellucida (pink, left, and red, above) of the egg. Eventually one sperm breaks through. It is taken into the egg through its outer membrane. As this happens, the sperm's tail falls off. Immediately, changes inside the egg mean that no other sperm can enter it. The nucleus inside the sperm's head fuses with the egg's nucleus. The newly formed nucleus contains all the information needed to make a new individual human being. Fertilization is complete.

Nucleus of sperm

Sperm

Nucleus of egg

Egg

Hazardous journey

On average 400 million sperm are released into the vagina during sexual intercourse. A few thousand sperm make it through the cervix into the uterus. A few hundred survive the hazardous two-to-seven-hour journey from the vagina to reach the fallopian tubes. Here an egg may, or may not, be present.

CONCEPTION & IMPLANTATION

After fertilization the fertilized egg continues on its journey along the fallopian tube toward the uterus. When, after several days, the fertilized egg arrives in the uterus, it attaches itself to the lining. This is called implantation. The period of time from fertilization to implantation is called conception. During conception the fertilized egg undergoes changes that mark the beginning of a new life.

As the fertilized egg is wafted along the fallopian tube, it divides into two. This is the first of millions of cell divisions that eventually produce a baby. Repeated divisions soon produce a mass of cells that arrives in the uterus and implants in the inner lining.

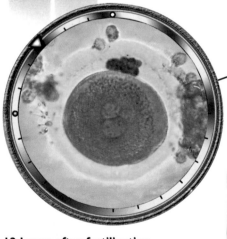

12 hours after fertilization
Inside this fertilized egg are two nuclei: one from the sperm and one from the egg. Soon they will join together so that the cell has a full set of chromosomes. These contain all the instructions necessary to produce a new human.

30 hours after fertilization
As the fertilized egg continues its journey toward the uterus, it divides into two cells. From this stage until implantation the fertilized egg is called a conceptus.

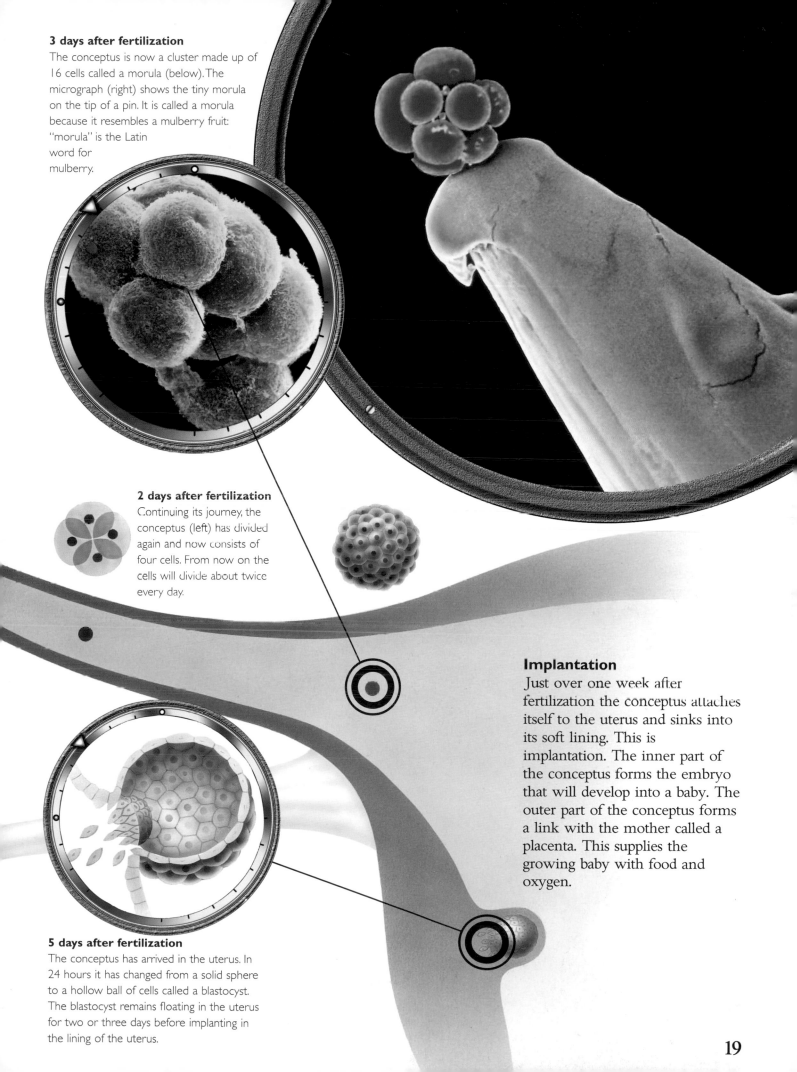

3 days after fertilization
The conceptus is now a cluster made up of 16 cells called a morula (below). The micrograph (right) shows the tiny morula on the tip of a pin. It is called a morula because it resembles a mulberry fruit: "morula" is the Latin word for mulberry.

2 days after fertilization
Continuing its journey, the conceptus (left) has divided again and now consists of four cells. From now on the cells will divide about twice every day.

Implantation
Just over one week after fertilization the conceptus attaches itself to the uterus and sinks into its soft lining. This is implantation. The inner part of the conceptus forms the embryo that will develop into a baby. The outer part of the conceptus forms a link with the mother called a placenta. This supplies the growing baby with food and oxygen.

5 days after fertilization
The conceptus has arrived in the uterus. In 24 hours it has changed from a solid sphere to a hollow ball of cells called a blastocyst. The blastocyst remains floating in the uterus for two or three days before implanting in the lining of the uterus.

HOW THE EMBRYO DEVELOPS

In the seven weeks that follow implantation the embryo develops rapidly. The growing embryo floats in a bag of fluid. This, and the thick lining of the uterus, keep the embryo warm and protect it from knocks and bumps.

Growth occurs because the embryo's cells are constantly dividing and expanding. But changing shape and developing into a human being need more than cell division. As new cells appear, they are destined to form particular tissues inside the embryo. Some, for example, become muscle, while others form nerves or bone. During its development the embryo changes from a hollow ball of cells into a tiny human being with arms and legs and a beating heart. Eight weeks after fertilization the strawberry-sized embryo is called a fetus.

Embryo at five weeks
Five weeks after fertilization the embryo is about 0.5 inches (1.2 centimeters) long. A tube called the umbilical cord is its lifeline, feeding blood from the mother.

Inside the uterus
Initially, the embryo is very small in relation to the size of the uterus. But during the nine months of pregnancy it will grow enough to make the uterus expand.

Embryo at 4 weeks
Four weeks after fertilization the embryo is just 0.2 inches (5 millimeters) long. It is, however, 10,000 times heavier than the fertilized egg that produced it! Inside the tiny embryo its major organs are forming. The heart starts to beat. And the umbilical cord forms. This will link the embryo to the disklike placenta that connects it to its mother.

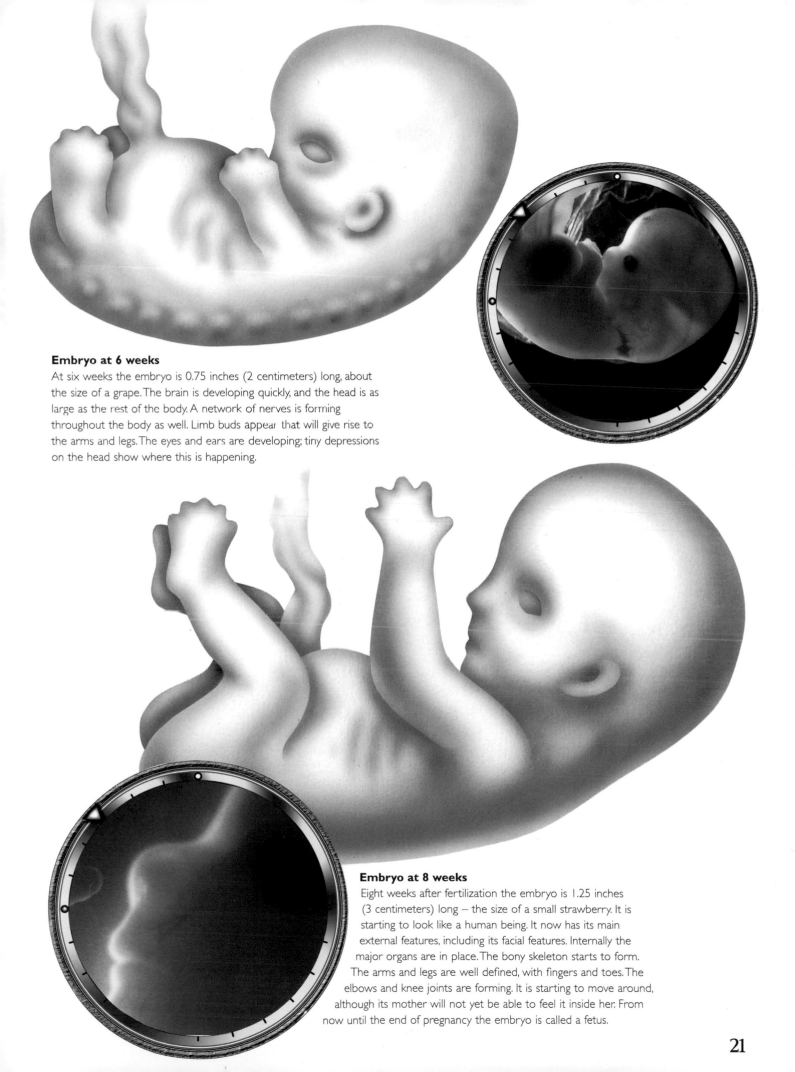

Embryo at 6 weeks

At six weeks the embryo is 0.75 inches (2 centimeters) long, about the size of a grape. The brain is developing quickly, and the head is as large as the rest of the body. A network of nerves is forming throughout the body as well. Limb buds appear that will give rise to the arms and legs. The eyes and ears are developing; tiny depressions on the head show where this is happening.

Embryo at 8 weeks

Eight weeks after fertilization the embryo is 1.25 inches (3 centimeters) long – the size of a small strawberry. It is starting to look like a human being. It now has its main external features, including its facial features. Internally the major organs are in place. The bony skeleton starts to form. The arms and legs are well defined, with fingers and toes. The elbows and knee joints are forming. It is starting to move around, although its mother will not yet be able to feel it inside her. From now until the end of pregnancy the embryo is called a fetus.

HOW THE FETUS DEVELOPS

After two months as an embryo the developing human is called a fetus. Over the next seven months, the fetus will increase in weight dramatically — from 1 ounce (25 grams) at 8 weeks, to around 7 pounds (3 kilograms) at birth. The middle months of pregnancy see the fetus becoming more and more like a tiny human.

Twelve weeks after fertilization the fetus is about 3 inches (8 centimeters) long. It looks more human than it did before, but its head is still large in proportion to the rest of its body. The 16-week-old fetus is 6 inches (16 centimeters) long — just big enough to make its mother look pregnant. Its body is covered with fine hair called lanugo. It can suck its thumb, move around, and it has its own fingerprints. By 20 weeks it is 8 inches (20 centimeters) long. Doctors usually carry out tests during these weeks to make sure that the fetus is growing normally. One of these tests is the ultrasound scan that allows the doctor to "see" the fetus.

Fetus at 12 weeks

At 12 weeks a mother's uterus is starting to swell, but its shape stays the same. The fetus's arms and legs are small but fully formed, with fingers and toes, each with its miniature nail. The fetus's muscles have developed enough for it to curl its toes, make a fist, and frown.

Umbilical cord

This view inside the uterus shows the fingers and umbilical cord of a 10-week-old fetus. Inside the cord you can see the spiralling blood vessels that carry food and oxygen from its mother.

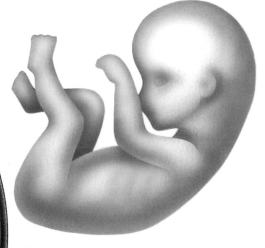

Face of a fetus

The facial features of this 12-week-old fetus are now clearly visible. The eyelids have formed and are closed over the eyes. Ears can be seen on the side of the head, and nostrils on the nose. The lips can now be opened and closed to suck in liquid.

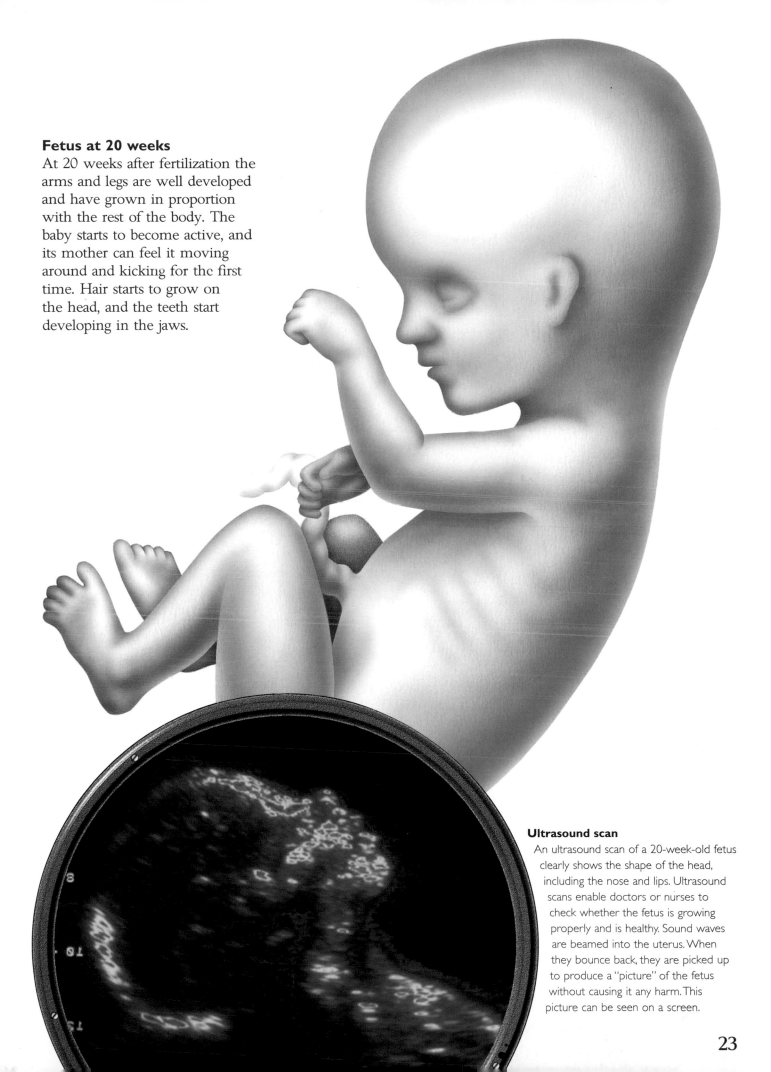

Fetus at 20 weeks

At 20 weeks after fertilization the arms and legs are well developed and have grown in proportion with the rest of the body. The baby starts to become active, and its mother can feel it moving around and kicking for the first time. Hair starts to grow on the head, and the teeth start developing in the jaws.

Ultrasound scan

An ultrasound scan of a 20-week-old fetus clearly shows the shape of the head, including the nose and lips. Ultrasound scans enable doctors or nurses to check whether the fetus is growing properly and is healthy. Sound waves are beamed into the uterus. When they bounce back, they are picked up to produce a "picture" of the fetus without causing it any harm. This picture can be seen on a screen.

GETTING READY FOR BIRTH

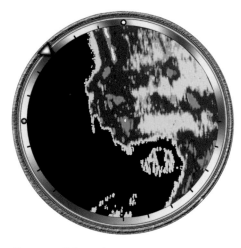

Fetus at 24 weeks
This colored ultrasound scan shows the head of a fetus 24 weeks after fertilization. The fetus is now 10 inches (25 centimeters) long. Its muscles are well formed. It can kick vigorously. Its skin is made waterproof by a white waxy substance called vernix. It may even cough and hiccup.

During the final months of pregnancy the fetus continues to grow. It is now preparing for its arrival into the outside world. The part of the fetus's brain that deals with intelligence and personality grows bigger and more complex. The fetus makes facial expressions such as smiling and frowning. Its eyelids open and close, and it can now see. It can hear voices and may distinguish between familiar and unfamiliar sounds. Its taste buds form so that it can taste its surroundings. It has periods of sleeping and times when it is awake.

The fetus's mother is fully aware of the offspring inside her. She can feel it tossing and turning and kicking. Her "bulge" is getting still bigger. As in the earlier months of pregnancy, the fetus is enclosed inside its protective environment. It floats in amniotic fluid within the transparent balloon formed by the amnion. This liquid cushion absorbs any sudden shocks and jolts. Food and oxygen are still passed through the placenta, which provides a vital link between fetus and mother.

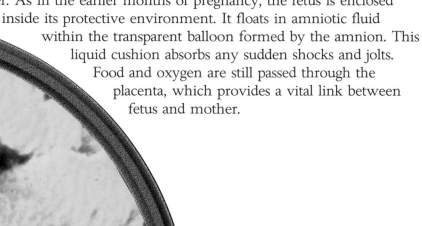

Life support system
The placenta is a flat, spongy organ attached to the lining of the uterus. It forms between the developing fetus and its mother. Inside the placenta the blood vessels of the fetus and those of the mother come into very close contact, but they do not meet. Food and oxygen pass from the mother's blood vessels into those of the fetus; carbon dioxide and other wastes pass in the opposite direction so that they can be got rid of. The umbilical cord, up to 24 inches (60 centimeters) long, links the placenta and fetus. It contains arteries and veins. These carry food and oxygen from the placenta to the fetus and wastes in the opposite direction.

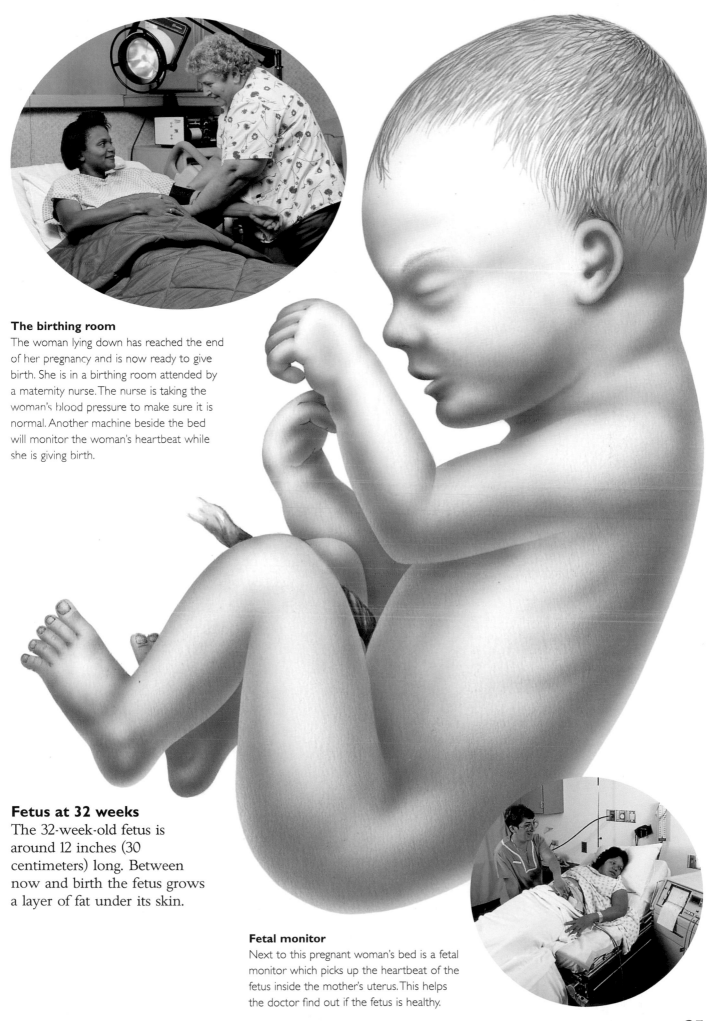

The birthing room

The woman lying down has reached the end of her pregnancy and is now ready to give birth. She is in a birthing room attended by a maternity nurse. The nurse is taking the woman's blood pressure to make sure it is normal. Another machine beside the bed will monitor the woman's heartbeat while she is giving birth.

Fetus at 32 weeks

The 32-week-old fetus is around 12 inches (30 centimeters) long. Between now and birth the fetus grows a layer of fat under its skin.

Fetal monitor

Next to this pregnant woman's bed is a fetal monitor which picks up the heartbeat of the fetus inside the mother's uterus. This helps the doctor find out if the fetus is healthy.

How Labor Begins

Some 266 days after fertilization took place the fetus is at full term. This means it is fully developed and facing head downward, ready to be born.

Mothers often feel increasingly uncomfortable because of the size of the fetus inside them and impatient for the birth to take place.

The sequence of events that leads to birth is called labor. It has three stages. During the first stage the muscular walls of the uterus start to contract. At first the contractions occur every 15 to 30 minutes. But they become more and more frequent until they are happening every two to three minutes. These contractions are triggered by hormones released by the fetus, by the placenta, and by the pituitary gland. The contractions push the fetus downward. At the same time, the cervix widens to allow the baby's head to pass into it. Eventually the amnion breaks and releases the amniotic fluid down the vagina. This is called "breaking the waters."

The first stage of labor lasts between 12 and 14 hours on average. Once it is completed, birth will soon follow.

Final checks

The time before birth can be a difficult one for some mothers. It is important to check a number of things, especially blood pressure, which must not get too high. By monitoring the mother's body during the birth, doctors and nurses can be sure of taking immediate action if there are any problems.

Fetus at full term

At full term the fetus (right) lies in the uterus with its head downward, ready to be born. Most of the waxy vernix that protected its skin has gone. So too has the soft lanugo hair that covered its body.

Ready for birth

This remarkable picture (right) shows a side view of a woman soon to give birth. On the left you can see the mother's abdomen bulging outward. Within it is the fetus itself, facing downward and ready for birth. On the right are the bones of the mother's backbone.

First stage of labor

The uterus contracts to push the baby out. The cervix widens to allow the baby to pass through it (left). As the uterus contracts, the baby's head is pushed into the opening. The amniotic sac breaks, releasing the amniotic fluid.

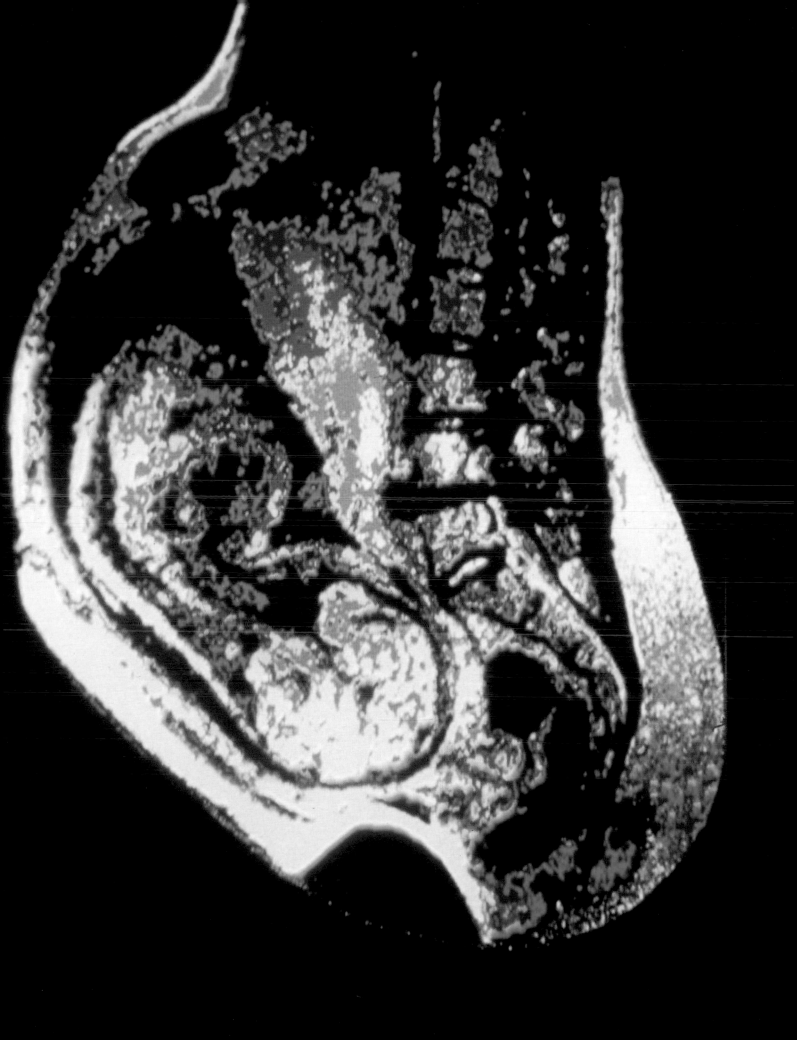

Birth

The second stage of labor is birth itself. The muscles in the wall of the uterus are now contracting strongly every two to three minutes, with each contraction lasting about one minute. The contractions push the baby headfirst along the birth canal, as the vagina is called at this time.

Although the cervix has widened, the baby must still be squeezed through a very narrow opening. To get through, the baby's head is actually slightly squashed temporarily.

Eventually the head emerges, closely followed by the rest of the body, and the baby is born. The birth usually takes less than an hour. When it emerges into the outside world, the baby leaves behind a warm and dark environment where it has been floating in liquid. It is now surrounded by light and noise, and the temperature has changed. The baby takes its first breaths, and its lungs expand for the first time. It cries and responds to its surroundings. The umbilical cord is clamped by the midwife or doctor and cut.

About 15 minutes after the birth the third and final stage of labor is completed. The uterus pushes the placenta – now called the afterbirth – out of the uterus. It is then discarded.

Second stage of labor
Contractions of the uterus wall push the baby headfirst out of the uterus and along the birth canal. The baby's head is turned so that it faces backward. This enables it to pass through the narrow opening between the bones of its mother's pelvis.

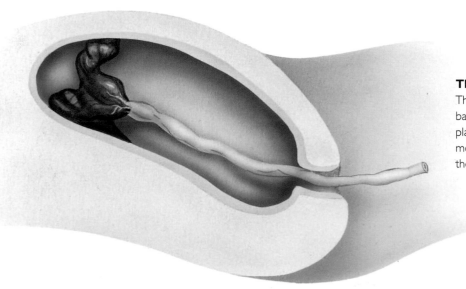

Third stage of labor
The uterus continues to contract after the baby is born. These contractions push the placenta, now no longer needed, out of the mother's uterus through her vagina. This is the afterbirth.

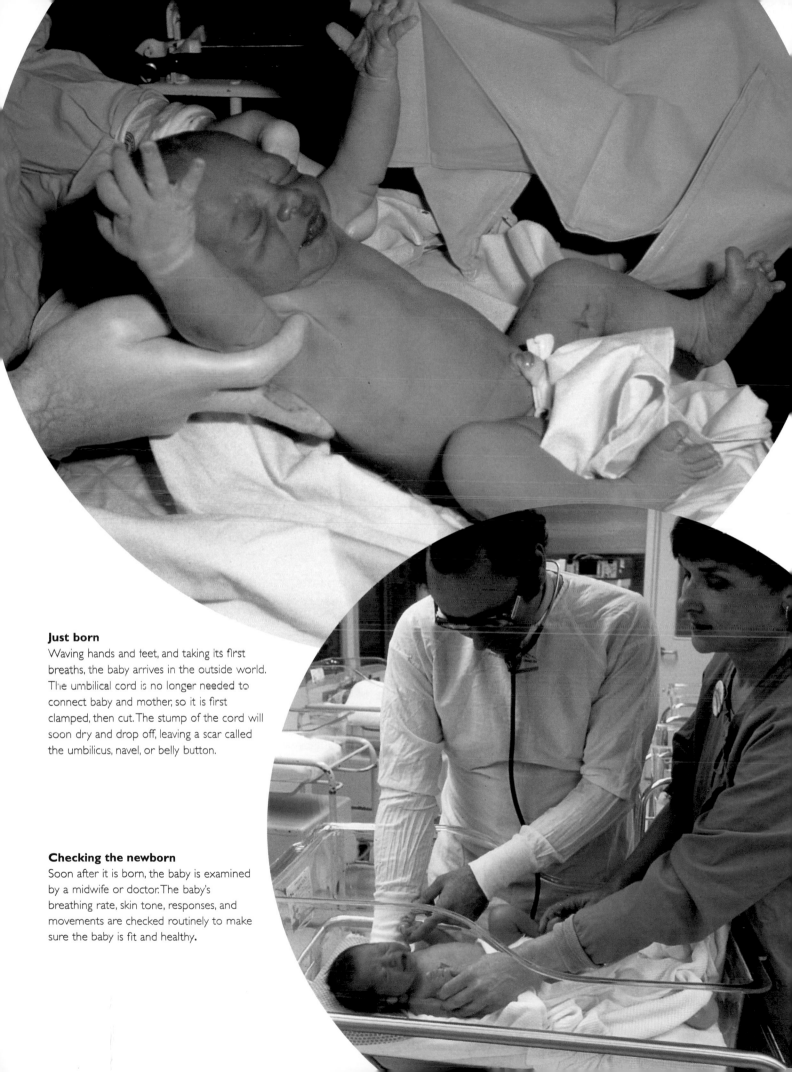

Just born
Waving hands and feet, and taking its first breaths, the baby arrives in the outside world. The umbilical cord is no longer needed to connect baby and mother, so it is first clamped, then cut. The stump of the cord will soon dry and drop off, leaving a scar called the umbilicus, navel, or belly button.

Checking the newborn
Soon after it is born, the baby is examined by a midwife or doctor. The baby's breathing rate, skin tone, responses, and movements are checked routinely to make sure the baby is fit and healthy.

TWINS

Most women have one baby at a time. But sometimes two or more babies are born at once. Two babies — twins — are born in one out of every 80 pregnancies.

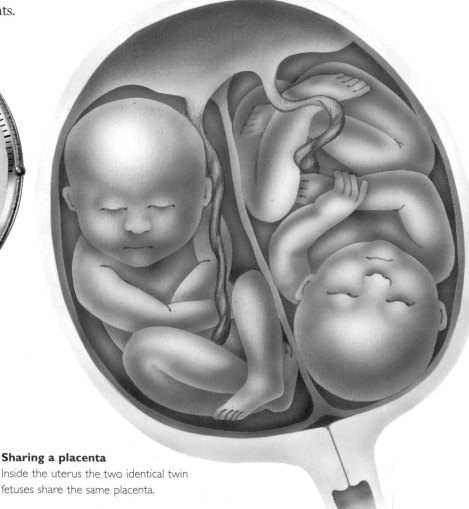

Most twins — about seven out of every 10 pairs — are nonidentical twins. The two individuals may look very different. They may be the same sex or brother and sister. The reason for this is that each one comes from a different fertilized egg. Each fertilized egg contains slightly different genetic information — the information supplied by parents in their egg and sperm, and needed to construct a new human being. Because each egg and sperm are different, every individual produced by a single egg and sperm looks different.

About three out of 20 pairs of twins are identical. They look like each other and are always the same sex. Each twin comes from the same fertilized egg. Unusually, the fertilized egg divides into two separate cells. Each one develops into a fetus. Because they come from the same fertilized egg, identical twins share the same genetic information. They may develop quite different characters as they get older, however. And they do not share the same fingerprints.

Identical twins

These identical twins look the same and may be very difficult to tell apart. Identical twins are always the same sex — either two boys or two girls.

How identical twins form

An egg has been released from the ovary and is fertilized by a single sperm. The fertilized egg divides for the first time. The two cells it produces, unusually, separate. Each cell then develops into a fetus. Because each cell contains identical genetic information, the two fetuses are identical.

Sharing a placenta

Inside the uterus the two identical twin fetuses share the same placenta.

Fraternal twins

Fraternal twins are the same age but otherwise look just like any other brothers or sisters. Fraternal twins may be the same sex or different sexes.

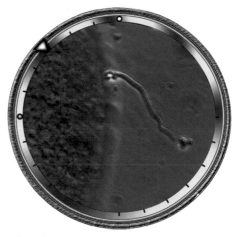

How fraternal twins are formed
Two eggs are released at the same time from one or both ovaries. Each egg is fertilized by a different sperm. The two fertilized eggs contain different genetic information. Because of this the two twins are not identical.

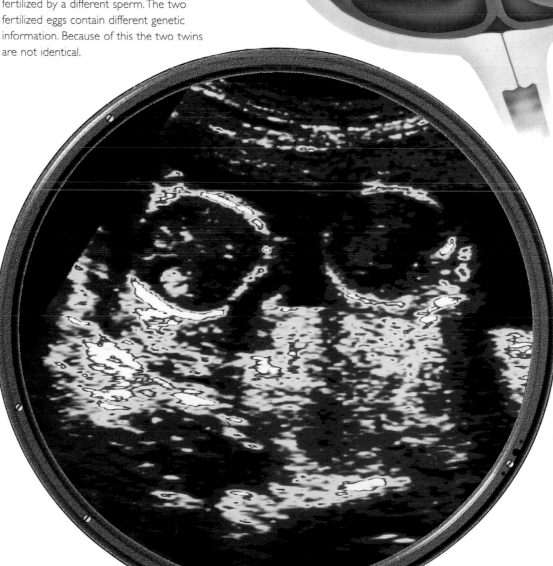

Independent existence
Inside the uterus fraternal twins develop separately. They do not share the same placenta.

Identical twins
This scan shows two identical twins developing side by side in the uterus. Because they developed from the same egg, they share the same placenta. Often, one will grow at the expense of the other.

CHROMOSOMES & CELL DIVISION

The human body is made up of billions of cells. Inside every cell is a control center called the nucleus, and inside each nucleus there are thread-like structures called chromosomes. The chromosomes carry all the instructions needed to build and run a human being, including the way we look. Body cells have 46 chromosomes, arranged in 23 pairs. In each pair one chromosome comes from the father and one from the mother. A chromosome is made of many smaller units called genes. There are about 100,000 genes in every cell nucleus. Each gene contains the instructions for one particular feature.

As body cells wear out, certain cells in each tissue make new ones to replace them. They do this by a type of cell division called mitosis. In mitosis a cell divides into two cells, each with the same chromosomes and genes as the original cell.

A different type of cell division takes place in the testes and the ovaries. This is called meiosis. This produces sex cells – sperm and eggs. Sex cells contain just one set of chromosomes: 23 chromosomes – half the normal number.

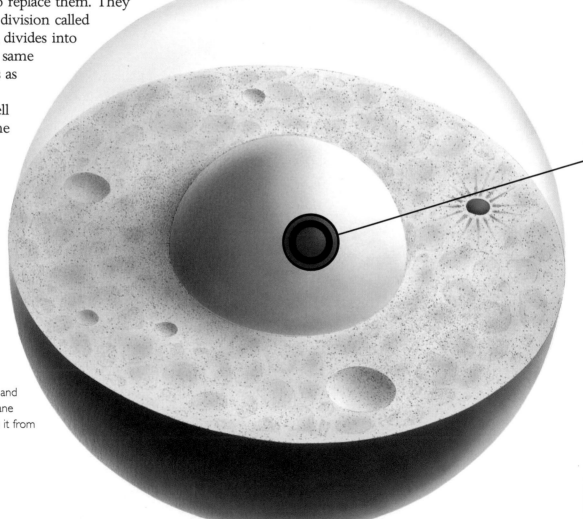

Human body cell
This human body cell has two main parts: the outer cytoplasm and the inner nucleus. A cell membrane surrounds the cell and separates it from its surroundings.

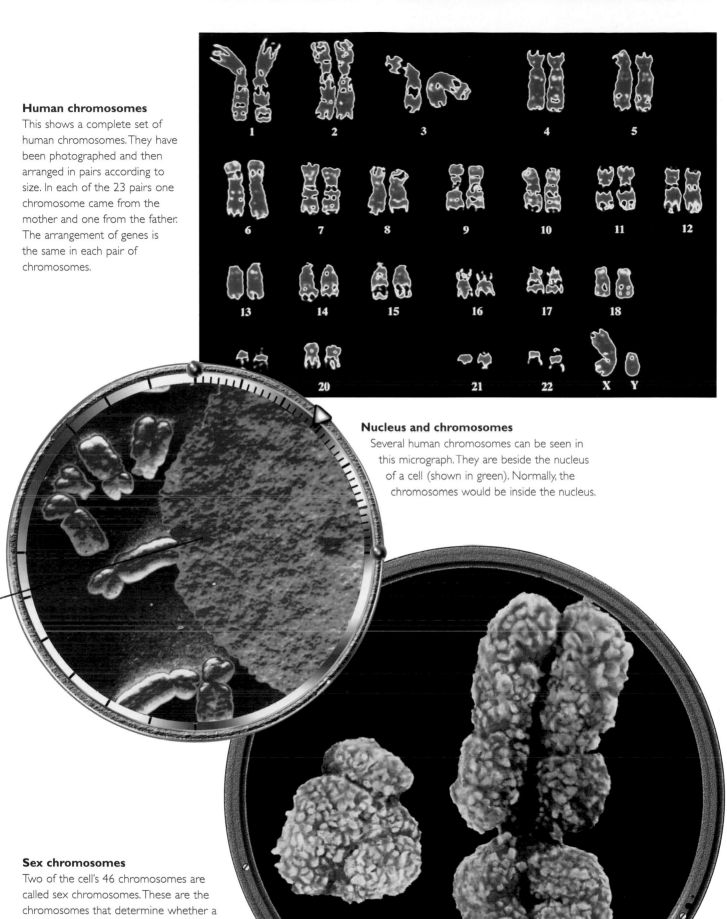

Human chromosomes

This shows a complete set of human chromosomes. They have been photographed and then arranged in pairs according to size. In each of the 23 pairs one chromosome came from the mother and one from the father. The arrangement of genes is the same in each pair of chromosomes.

Nucleus and chromosomes

Several human chromosomes can be seen in this micrograph. They are beside the nucleus of a cell (shown in green). Normally, the chromosomes would be inside the nucleus.

Sex chromosomes

Two of the cell's 46 chromosomes are called sex chromosomes. These are the chromosomes that determine whether a baby will be a boy or a girl. In girls the sex chromosomes are identical. In boys they are different, as you can see in this micrograph. One is long, while the other is small and squat.

A BOY OR A GIRL?

How is the sex of a new baby-to-be determined? Out of the 23 pairs of chromosomes in all its body cells, one pair is slightly different. This pair is called the sex chromosomes because it decides whether the baby will be a boy or a girl.

There are two sex chromosomes called X and Y because of their shape. A person with two X-chromosomes is female. A person with one X- and one Y-chromosome is male. Eggs and sperm carry only one set of chromosomes and, therefore, only one sex chromosome. A woman's eggs can carry only an X-chromosome. A man's sperm can carry an X- or a Y-chromosome. So, at fertilization the sex of the future child depends on which sex chromosome the sperm is carrying. For every baby the chances of that being X or Y are 50:50.

Chromosomes and sex
Most chromosomes are roughly X-shaped. But one of the two sex chromosomes may be Y-shaped, as you can see in the top of this micrograph. A baby who has a Y-shaped chromosome in his body cells will be a boy.

XX – it's a girl
Egg and sperm each have one sex chromosome. The egg's is always X-shaped. But the sperm's may be either an X or a Y. If the sperm that fertilizes the egg has an X-chromosome, the baby will have two X-chromosomes and will be a girl. A girl always has two X-chromosomes, one from her father and one from her mother.

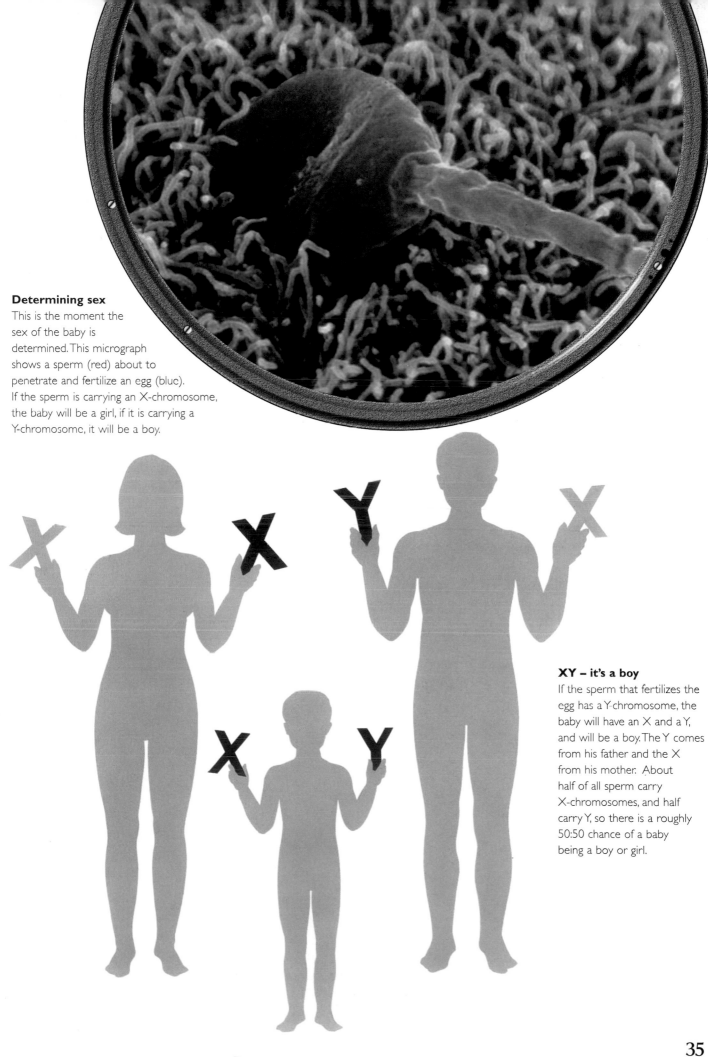

Determining sex

This is the moment the sex of the baby is determined. This micrograph shows a sperm (red) about to penetrate and fertilize an egg (blue). If the sperm is carrying an X-chromosome, the baby will be a girl, if it is carrying a Y-chromosome, it will be a boy.

XY – it's a boy

If the sperm that fertilizes the egg has a Y-chromosome, the baby will have an X and a Y, and will be a boy. The Y comes from his father and the X from his mother. About half of all sperm carry X-chromosomes, and half carry Y, so there is a roughly 50:50 chance of a baby being a boy or girl.

GENETICS & HEREDITY

We all belong to the human race. As such, we are all identifiable as human beings. But there are also many differences between individuals. At the same time, we usually resemble other family members much more than we do unrelated people. And we most closely resemble our closest relatives – our parents and brothers and sisters.

Family resemblance
These children received half of their genes from each of their parents. A quarter of their genes came originally from each of their four grandparents. The "package" of genes carried in each sex cell varies. This means that the children of one set of parents may resemble each other but never look exactly the same (unless they are identical twins).

The reason for this is that we inherit a set of genes from each of our parents. These genes are found on the chromosomes carried by the egg and sperm. The genes carried on the chromosomes are instructions that ensure we appear human and resemble our parents, but they also give us a stamp of individuality. The way in which characteristics and features are passed on from parents to children is called heredity.

The genes we inherit are in pairs: one from mother and one from father. But not all genes carry out their instructions. Take the genes that control eye color, for example. A person may inherit two genes that give the same instructions for blue eye color: he has blue eyes. Or he may inherit one gene that produces blue eye color and one gene that produces brown. In this case he has brown eyes: the brown eye gene carries out its instructions, while the blue eye gene does not.

Where a gene carries out its instructions, it is called dominant; where it does not carry out its instructions, it is called recessive. The combination of dominant and recessive genes in a person's chromosomes produces the unique individual that he or she is. The study ofhow genes are passed on and work together to make an individual is called genetics.

Generation to generation
Here you can see several generations of one family, from great grandparents to great grandchildren (right). The youngest children have genes that were passed down to them from their great grandmother through one of their grandparents and one of their parents. An even closer family likeness is shown between the grandmother, mother, and daughter in the photograph on the far right.

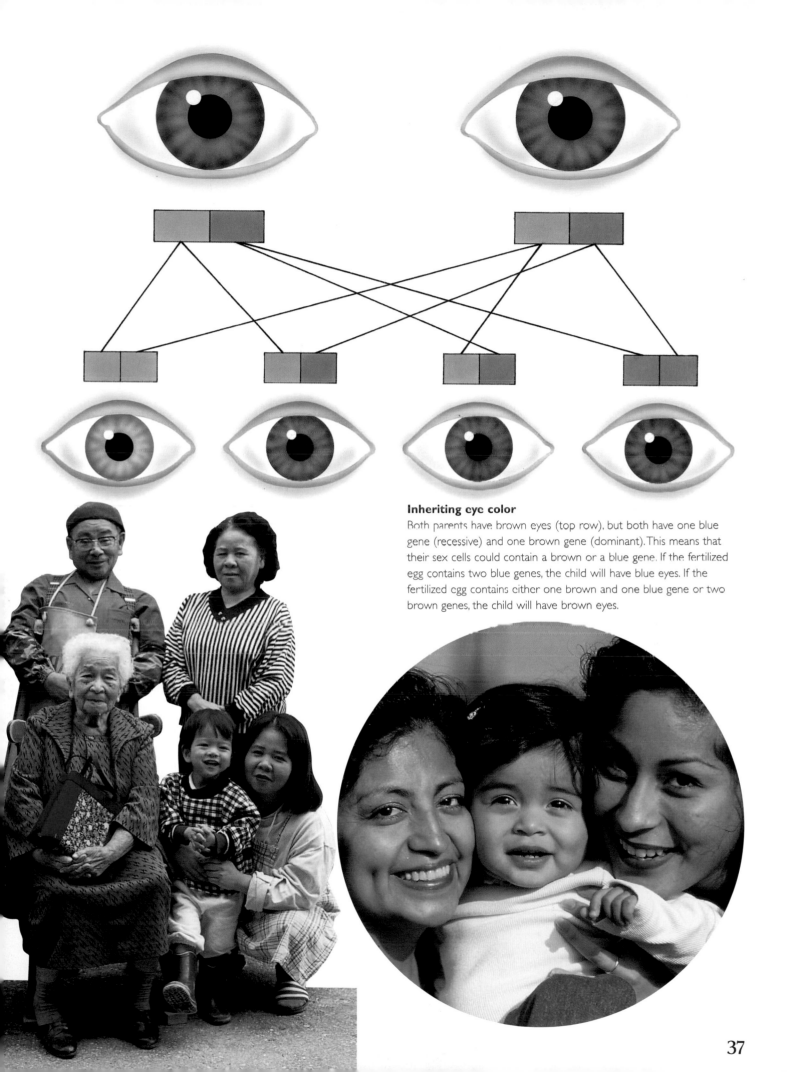

Inheriting eye color
Both parents have brown eyes (top row), but both have one blue gene (recessive) and one brown gene (dominant). This means that their sex cells could contain a brown or a blue gene. If the fertilized egg contains two blue genes, the child will have blue eyes. If the fertilized egg contains either one brown and one blue gene or two brown genes, the child will have brown eyes.

FROM BABY TO CHILD

Mother and baby
Human babies need constant care and feeding during their first three months. Then there are many years of care and teaching as they grow up. In fact, it can take 20 years before a child is fully independent.

Growing through childhood
Children grow and learn from the minute they are born. This sequence shows how the average weight and height of a child changes. It also shows what a child can do at each age.

Humans take a long time to develop into adults. When a baby is born, it needs constant care and attention. As the child gets older, the amount of care decreases, but most children need to be protected and nurtured by their parents through the first 15–20 years of life.

All children grow rapidly in their first year, more slowly after that, but then rapidly again in their teens before growth stops altogether.

As children grow in size, their bodies change in shape because bones grow at different rates. A baby's head, for example, is about one-quarter of its length; a teenager's head is just one-eighth of its length.

As each year passes and children grow, they develop new skills and abilities. The brain grows more complex as more connections develop between the billions of brain cells. New behaviors and movements are rehearsed and learned. A newborn baby cannot move far or talk, but a child of three can say short sentences and walk. By the age of eight most children can run, draw, sing, read, write, and ride a bicycle. The children on these pages show what we can do at each age. Heights and weights given are for boys. Girls are slightly shorter and lighter.

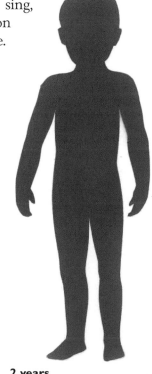

1 month
Weight 9.1 pounds (4.1 kg); height 21.2 inches (53.8 cm).

At one month a baby spends much of her day asleep. She is dependent on her parents for warmth and food. She will cry for attention if hungry, cold, or in pain. She can recognize familiar faces, such as her mother's.

6 months
Weight 16.7 pounds (7.6 kg); height 26.1 inches (66.3 cm).

By six months an infant can sit on a chair and reach for objects. He communicates with gurgles and chuckles but will still cry when hungry or in pain.

1 year
Weight 22.2 pounds (10.1 kg); height 29.6 inches (75.2 cm).

This one-year-old can pull herself up and is starting to walk. She can say simple words but understands more than she can say. She can pick up objects between her thumb and first finger and pass objects when someone asks her.

2 years
Weight 27.7 pounds (12.6 kg); height 34.4 inches (87.4 cm).

A two-year-old child's arms and legs are much longer than an infant's. He can walk and run easily. He picks up objects while standing up. He may talk in short sentences and sing songs. He enjoys following stories in his favorite books.

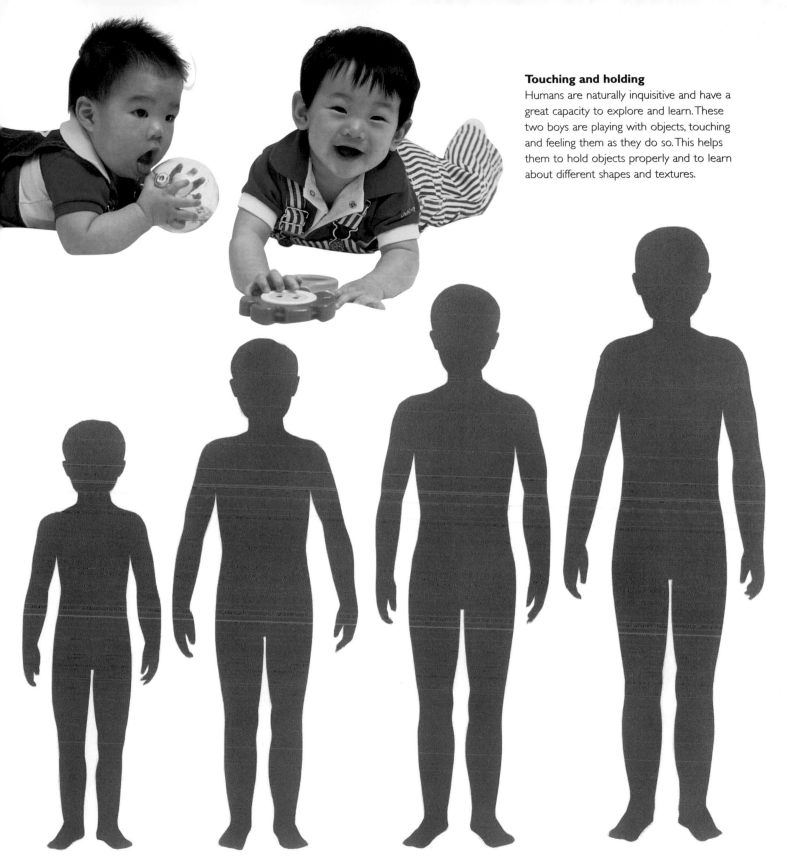

Touching and holding

Humans are naturally inquisitive and have a great capacity to explore and learn. These two boys are playing with objects, touching and feeling them as they do so. This helps them to hold objects properly and to learn about different shapes and textures.

4 years

Weight 36.4 pounds (16.5 kg); height 40.7 inches (1.03 m).

A four-year-old can hold conversations and will ask lots of questions. She can sing and speak with fluency. She runs easily and can hop on one foot. She can draw simple pictures of people: usually a round body with stick arms and legs.

6 years

Weight 48.3 pounds (21.9 kg); height 46.3 inches (1.2 m).

A six-year-old can play simple sports and jump over a rope. She can read her own books and can write simple words. When asked, she can match similar objects.

8 years

Weight 60.1 pounds (27.3 kg); height 51.2 inches (1.3 m).

Many eight-year-olds can read and write with ease. They communicate clearly and are beginning to reason about things. They can balance more easily and can ride a bicycle.

10 years

Weight 71.9 pounds (32.6 kg); height 55.2 inches (1.45 m).

Ten-year-olds are reaching the end of their childhood and are soon to become teenagers. Their bodies are beginning the changes that take them from being children to young adults.

Puberty timeline

9.5-14.5 years
- Breasts start to develop
- The growth spurt occurs
- Armpit hairs grow
- Armpit sweat glands start working
- The uterus grows

11-14 years
- Periods start
- Pubic hairs appear
- Oil glands in the skin become more active
- Fat deposits under the skin produce a more rounded shape

GROWING UP: GIRLS

When a girl reaches her early teens, her body starts to grow and change very rapidly. This is puberty. It is the time when a girl becomes a young woman. Her reproductive system begins working. She will now be capable of reproducing and having children.

CHANGES IN BODY SHAPE
During puberty growth accelerates rapidly, and a girl's shape changes. Her breasts grow, and her nipples get larger. Her hips widen, and her whole body shape becomes more rounded.

10 years

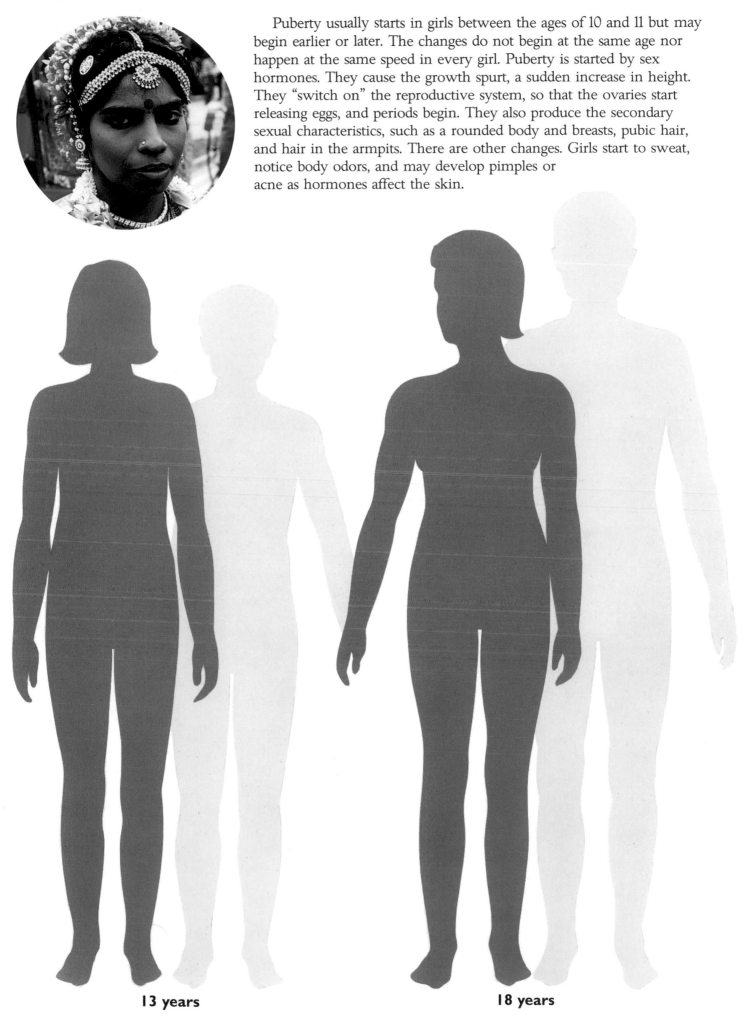

Puberty usually starts in girls between the ages of 10 and 11 but may begin earlier or later. The changes do not begin at the same age nor happen at the same speed in every girl. Puberty is started by sex hormones. They cause the growth spurt, a sudden increase in height. They "switch on" the reproductive system, so that the ovaries start releasing eggs, and periods begin. They also produce the secondary sexual characteristics, such as a rounded body and breasts, pubic hair, and hair in the armpits. There are other changes. Girls start to sweat, notice body odors, and may develop pimples or acne as hormones affect the skin.

13 years

18 years

GROWING UP: BOYS

11-12

- Testes grow
- Scrotum becomes darker and more wrinkly

12-13

- Penis grows longer and wider
- Pubic hair grows
- Armpit sweat glands start working
- The growth spurt begins

13-15

- Armpit and body hair starts growing
- Facial hair starts growing
- Oil glands in the skin become more active
- Testes produce sperm
- Sperm and semen may be released during ejaculation

14-15

- The voice "breaks" and becomes deeper

As he enters his teens, a boy's body grows and changes rapidly, just as a girl's does. Like her, he is going through puberty. His weight almost doubles, and he shoots up in height. He stops being a boy and becomes a young man. His reproductive system "switches on," so that he is now able to reproduce.

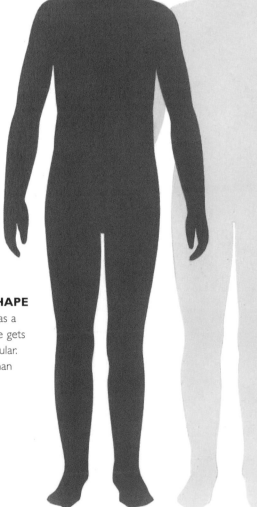

CHANGES IN BODY SHAPE
Body size and shape change as a boy goes through puberty. He gets taller, broader, and more muscular. His shoulders become wider than his hips. His penis and testes become larger.

10 years

In boys puberty usually begins between the ages of 13 and 14 but may be earlier or later. It is started by sex hormones, especially testosterone. They cause the growth spurt and "switch on" the reproductive system, so that the testes start releasing sperm. Hormones also produce the secondary sexual characteristics such as a muscular body, broad chest and shoulders, pubic hair, and a deep voice caused by the lengthening of the larynx (voice box) in the throat. Many young men grow hair on their body and face. As in girls, a boy's armpits produce a different kind of sweat, and they may also develop pimples.

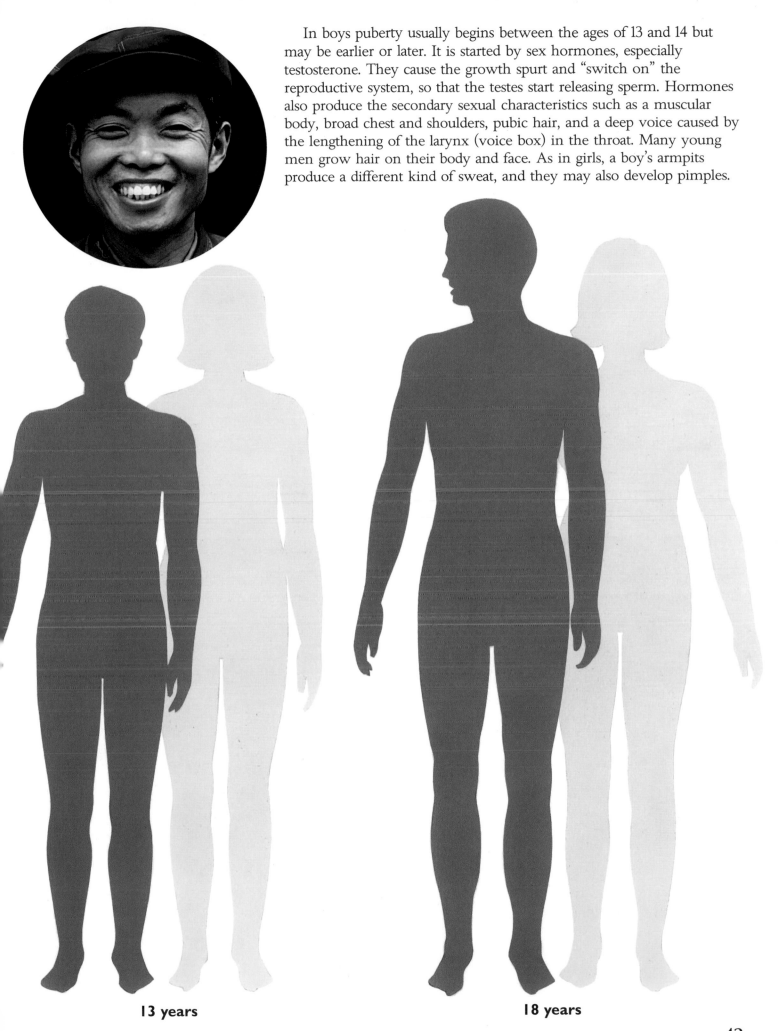

13 years

18 years

GETTING OLDER

Old but fit
There is no reason why old age has to mean that people are less healthy. This couple have stayed fit through daily physical work and by keeping plenty of interests in their life.

As we saw at the beginning of this book, none of us can live forever. Slowly but surely we get older, and as we do so, our bodies change until eventually our lives come to an end.

Between the ages of 45 and 55 the human body starts to age. The billions of cells that make up the body stop working as efficiently. The skin becomes less elastic and starts to wrinkle. Bones become more brittle and more likely to break. Muscles become smaller and lose some of their strength. The eyes and ears become less efficient at their jobs. Hair turns gray or white and may fall out. We lose height as our spine shortens, and we become more stooped.

Women between 45 and 55 stop releasing eggs from their ovaries and stop having periods. This time is called the menopause, and after it women can no longer have babies. Men continue to produce sperm into old age, although the numbers of sperm they make may decrease.

Despite these changes, many men and women stay fit and active in old age. The effects of aging can be slowed in many ways. Regular exercise, a good balanced diet, and a positive mental attitude help humans feel young even when old in years.

Aging features
As people age, their skin becomes less supple and elastic. As you can see here, these older women have wrinkled skin on their faces because of the process of aging.

Elder statesman
The changes brought on by aging can be seen in these two photographs of Nelson Mandela as a young lawyer and later in life as president of South Africa.

How old is old?
The average length of people's lives varies. In Japan you might expect to live into your 80s, while in some African countries 50 would seem very old. Where people have healthy diets and good health care, they live longer.

GLOSSARY

AMNION (Am-nee-on)
A "bag" of fluid – called amniotic fluid – that surrounds and protects the fetus during its development in the uterus.

CHROMOSOME (Krow-mow-sowm)
Threadlike structure in the nucleus of every body cell. Forty-six chromosomes in each cell carry all the instructions needed to make a person. Each chromosome is made of units called genes.

CONCEPTION (Kon-sep-shun)
Time from fertilization of an egg to implantation of the embryo in the lining of the uterus.

EMBRYO (Em-bree-oh)
The unborn baby in the earliest weeks of its growth and development after implantation and before it becomes a fetus.

EPIDIDYMIS (Ep-ee-did-ee-miss)
Long, coiled tube in which sperm mature after they are made in the testis.

FALLOPIAN TUBE (Fa-low-pee-ann)
Narrow tube that carries an egg after it has been released from an ovary to the uterus. Fertilization takes place in the fallopian tube.

FERTILIZATION (Fur-till-li-zay-shun)
The joining together of an egg and a sperm following sexual intercourse. The resulting fertilized egg develops into a baby.

FETUS (Fee-tuss)
A baby developing inside the uterus from eight weeks after fertilization to its birth.

GENES (Jeens)
Instructions stored on the chromosomes contained inside every body cell. Genes are passed on from parents to their children.

GENETICS (Jen-et-ticks)
The study of how characteristics are passed on from parents to children.

HORMONE (Hor-moan)
Chemical messenger released by a gland and carried by the blood. Hormones help control body activities, including reproduction.

IMPLANTATION (Imm-plarn-tay-shun)
Attachment of a fertilized egg to the lining of the uterus a few days after fertilization.

LABOR (Lay-bor)
Contraction of the muscles in the wall of the uterus that cause the baby to be born and pushed into the outside world.

MAMMARY GLANDS (Mamm-ar-ee)
Glands inside a woman's breasts that produce milk to feed her baby.

MENSTRUAL CYCLE (Men-stroo-al)
Regular sequence every month in which an egg is released from the ovary, and the lining of the uterus is lost during menstruation.

MENSTRUATION (Men-stroo-ay-shun)
Or period. The shedding of the lining of the uterus that happens once a month and lasts for about five days.

OVARY (Oh-va-ree)
Part of the female reproductive system which releases eggs and sex hormones.

OVULATION (O-vyoo-lay-shun)
The release of an egg from an ovary which occurs in the middle of each menstrual cycle.

OVUM/OVA
Term used by doctors to describe an egg/eggs, the female sex cells.

PENIS (Pee-niss)
Tubelike part of a man's reproductive system that he uses to introduce sperm into a woman's vagina during sexual intercourse.

PERIOD see menstruation.

PLACENTA (Pla-sen-tah)
Organ that links the blood supply of a mother to that of the developing fetus. The umbilical cord links the placenta to the fetus.

PROSTATE GLAND (Pross-tate)
Part of the male reproductive system that produces semen.

PUBERTY (Pyoo-ber-tee)
Part of a person's life – between the ages of 10 and 16 – when boys' and girls' bodies change as they become sexually mature and able to reproduce.

SCROTUM (Skrow-tum)
Bag of skin that holds the testes outside a man's body to keep them cool.

SEMEN (See-men)
Liquid made by the prostate and other glands that carries sperm and supplies them with food for their journey inside a woman's body.

SEX CELLS
General name given to sperm and eggs (ova).

SEX CHROMOSOMES
One of the 23 pairs of chromosomes. Sex chromosomes determine whether a baby will be male or female.

SEX HORMONES
Hormones that produce male and female sexual features, such as breasts and pubic hair.

SEXUAL INTERCOURSE
Intimate act during which a man places his penis in a woman's vagina and releases sperm.

SPERM
Male sex cells.

TESTIS/TESTES (Tess-tis/tess-tees)
Part of the male reproductive system that produces sperm and sex hormones.

UMBILICAL CORD (Um-bill-ee-kal)
Tube linking placenta and fetus, carrying food and oxygen to the fetus, and waste away.

UTERUS (Yoo-ter-us)
Part of the female reproductive system in which the baby develops.

VAGINA (Vaj-eye-na)
A muscular tube of female reproductive system that links the uterus to the outside of the body. The penis is placed inside the vagina during sexual intercourse.

SET INDEX

Volume numbers are in **bold**, followed by page numbers.

Acknowledgments

The publishers wish to thank the following for supplying photographs:

Alex Bartel/Science Photo Library (SPL) 26 (T); Biophoto Associates/SPL 6 (B), 33 (TR, BR); BSIP DuCloux/SPL 34 (TL); Clinical Radiology Dept. and Salisbury District Hospital/SPL 31 (B); CNRI/SPL 6 (TL), 16 (B), 24 (BL); Eye of Science/SPL 33 (CL); Don Fawcett/SPL 17 (CL); Gca-CNRI/SPL 24 (TL); John Greim/SPL 25 (TL); Keith/Custom Medical Stock Photo/SPL 22 (BL); David Leah/SPL 29 (T); Miles Kelly Archives 4 (TR), 40 (CL, BL), 41 (T), 42 (BL, CL), 43 (TR), 44 (BL, C, BR), 45 (BL, C, BR); Prof. P. Motta/Dept. of Anatomy/University "La Sapienza," Rome/SPL 7, 9 (BR), 15 (CR); Prof. P. Motta et al./SPL front cover (CL), 17 (T), 30 (BL); Profs. P. Motta, G. Macchiarelli and S. A. Nottola/SPL 9 (T); Profs. P. Motta and J. Van Blerkom/SPL 11 (T), 19 (TL); Larry Mulvehill/SPL 25 (BR); Dr. Yorgos Nikas/SPL 19 (TR); Panos Pictures 30 (TR), 36 (TR); Petit Format/Nestle/SPL 6 (CL), 11 (CL), 20 (TR), 21 (TR, BL), 22 (C); Petit Format/Prof. E. Symonds/SPL 27; D. Phillips/SPL 35 (T); Richard Rawlins/Custom Medical Stock Photo/SPL 31 (TL); Rex Features London 45 (TL, TR); P. H. Saada/Eurelios/SPL 23 (BL); David Scharf/SPL 12 (BL); Dr. Gerald Schatten/SPL 3 (TL), 15 (TL); Secchi, Lecaque, Roussel, UCLAF–CNRI/SPL back cover (BR), 3 (BL), 4 (BL), 13 (BR); Secchi, Lecaque–CNRI/SPL 3 (BR), 14-15 (BR); The Stock Market 36-7 (B), 37 (BR), 38 (TL), 39 (T); Smiljka Surla 44 (TL); Ed Young/SPL 29 (BR).